What Do Grown-Ups Do All Day?

by Virginie Morgand

WIDE EYED EDITIONS

Contents

Are you ready for an adventure?

Come with us and find out what grown-ups do...

Page 6

in our school

Page 18

on a construction site

Page 10

in a hospital

Page 22

when they go downtown

Page 14

on a farm

Page 26

in the theater

Page 30

in an action-packed job

Page 34

in a hotel

Page 38

in the great outdoors

Page 42

in a concert hall

Page 46

in a newsroom

Page 50

at the gym

Page 54

at a university

Page 58

at the airport

What do grown-ups do all day?

On this trip,
we are going to visit
14 different workplaces,
and in each place, we are
going to talk to eight people.

Each of the grown-ups you meet
can be seen doing his or her
job on the page before.
Can you spot them all?

Every day, lots of grown-ups all around us head out the door, and we don't see them again until later that evening...

But what do they do all day?

Many people go to a special workplace to do a job. A job can mean all kinds of things—it can mean working inside a building or working outside in the fresh air.

Over time, people develop different kinds of skills and abilities to do their job better. They might become excellent at making things with their hands, or good at using certain kinds of machinery, or using their brain to come up with new ideas and solutions to problems.

Join us on our adventure as we visit some very different workplaces to see what kinds of jobs people do all day. Which one do you like best?

Welcome to our school

When you start school, you will be given a good education by your teachers—and this will help you do a job when you are a grown-up yourself! And while math lessons and learning to read and write are important, at school you can also try art, drama, and sports, too.

What do grown-ups do in a school?

I am the PRINCIPAL. Welcome to our school!

I run the school and make sure everyone feels happy and safe.

I am a math TEACHER

In my classroom, you will learn to add and subtract...and lots more!

I am the LIBRARIAN

I am the GYM TEACHER

I look after the library and love to suggest good books for you to read.

I will play sports and games with you. Being active keeps you fit and healthy!

I am the
DRAMA
TEACHER

I am the
CUSTODIAN

I will teach you how to act, and help to put on the school play every year.

I work hard to keep the school clean and tidy, and a safe place for children.

I am a
STUDENT

I am the
MUSIC
TEACHER

Come and sing in my choir, or learn an instrument with me.

I'm not a grown-up…yet! I go to school every day with my friends.

Welcome to the hospital

If you are feeling sick, you might go to a hospital. Here, doctors and nurses work together to find out what is making you sick, and try to make you feel better, whether it be by fixing a broken bone or giving you medicine. But a hospital isn't just a place for sick patients—new babies are born here, too.

EMERGENCY

What do grown-ups do in a hospital?

I am a
DOCTOR

I try to find out what is making a patient sick, and help them feel better.

I am a
NURSE

I look after sick patients day and night, and give them their medicine.

I am a
PHYSICAL THERAPIST

I am the
PHARMACIST

I help patients recover through movement and special exercises.

I prepare medication that will help patients feel better and overcome illness.

I am an AMBULANCE DRIVER, and this is my speedy ambulance.

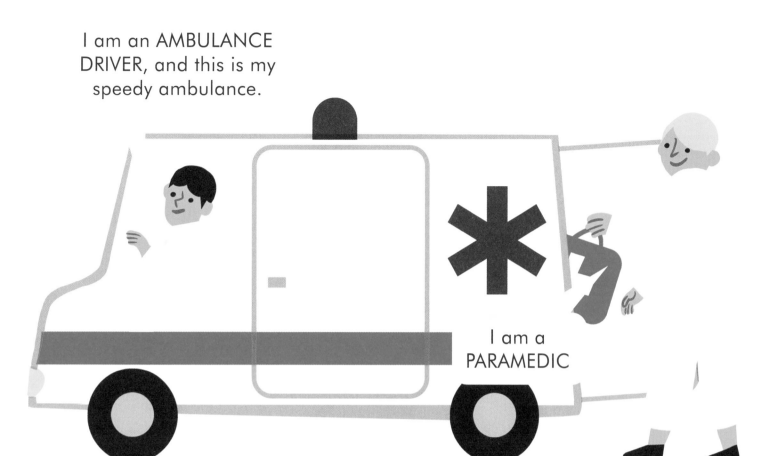

I am a PARAMEDIC

In an emergency, I drive the ambulance that will take a patient to the hospital.

I travel in the ambulance and give first aid to anyone who needs it.

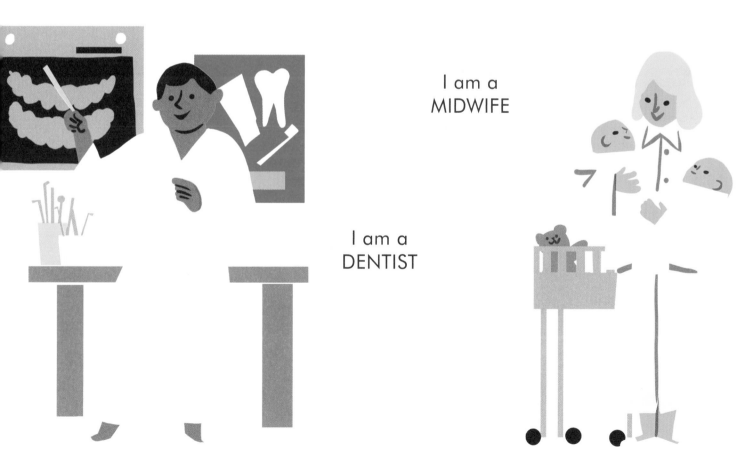

I am a MIDWIFE

I am a DENTIST

I take care of your teeth and gums—don't forget to floss at night!

I help deliver children into the world, and look after the newborn babies.

Welcome to the farm

Have you ever wondered where the food on your plate comes from? Nearly everything you eat—meat, vegetables, and even grain for your bread—was grown or reared by a farmer. A lot of care goes into looking after everything on a farm. Just take a look!

What do grown-ups do on a farm?

I am a
FARMER

I grow crops and raise animals to make the food that is on your plate!

I DRIVE the
TRACTOR

With my tractor, I plow the fields, sow seeds, and harvest the crops.

I am a
SHEPHERD

I am the
MECHANIC

I tend to the farm's flock of sheep. My sheepdog helps me to round them up!

I look after the machinery on the farm, and fix the tractor if it breaks.

I am a
VET

I am an animal doctor and make sure that the farm animals are healthy.

I MILK
the COWS

The milk that comes from cows also makes yogurt and cheese!

I am a
FARMHAND

I do all kinds of jobs to help the farmer, like feeding the animals.

I am a
GARDENER

I grow all kinds of fruits and vegetables, and keep the gardens looking pretty.

Welcome to the construction site

Whether you live in a small, historic village or a busy, modern city, everything around you was once built by skilled workers. As a building goes up, the area around it is called a construction site. If you visit one, hold on to your hard hat and look out for dangerous machines and heavy objects.

What do grown-ups do on a construction site?

I am an ARCHITECT

I plan and design buildings before they are constructed.

I am an ENGINEER

Using my expert knowledge, I make sure that buildings won't fall down!

I am an ELECTRICIAN

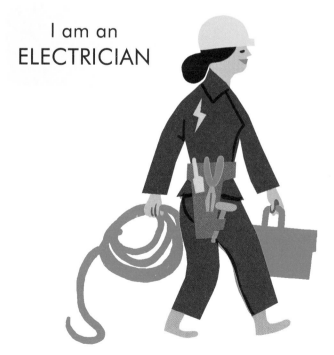

I put wires in the building, which provide you with electrical power and light.

I am a PLUMBER

I fix the pipes so that you have running water.

I am a LABORER

I am a PAINTER and
DECORATOR

I am strong and carry heavy loads, dig up
the ground—and demolish things!

Buildings look much nicer once
I've covered them with paint!

I am a
BRICKLAYER

I am a
CARPENTER

By putting up walls and tiling the roof,
I make a building warm and dry.

I am especially good at making
things out of wood.

Welcome downtown

It's lively downtown, full of hustle and bustle. Busy shoppers wander along Main Street—and the shopkeepers who work here keep their stores stocked full of the things that people have come here to buy!

greens

BAKERY

MEATS

lowers ✿ ↑SHOP BOOKS

23

What do grown-ups do when they go downtown?

I am a
BUTCHER

I have a shop where I sell meat to my customers, who take it home to cook.

I am a
BAKER

My bakery is full of the delicious breads and cakes that I have baked.

I run a
PRODUCE STAND

I sell all kinds of juicy fruits and ripe vegetables from my stand.

I am a
FLORIST

I make beautiful bouquets of flowers for people, which I sell from my stand.

I work in a
BOOKSHOP

I have shelves full of books in my shop,
and I can find the right one for everyone!

I am a
HAIRDRESSER

Come to my salon and I will make you
feel special with a new haircut.

I am a
SHOP
ASSISTANT

I am a
SHOPPER

As you wander through the shop, I make
sure you can find what you need.

I am out for a busy day of shopping—
I have lots of things on my shopping list!

Welcome to the theater

Going to the theater is a real treat! The actors there will make you laugh, cry, and sit on the edge of your seat as the drama unfolds. But putting on a performance takes a whole team of people behind the scenes who create costumes, scenery, sound effects, and lighting to transport you to another world.

What do grown-ups do in the theater?

I am an
ACTOR

I act the part of a character in a play…
and I have lots of lines to remember!

I am a
DIRECTOR

I give instructions to the actors during rehearsals
to make sure the play turns out well.

I am a
MAKEUP
ARTIST

I help the actors transform themselves to
play their part by putting their makeup on.

I am a SET
DESIGNER

I design the stage to show the
audience where the play is set.

I am a
COSTUME
DESIGNER

The clothes that actors wear onstage are called costumes—and I have designed them all!

I am a
PLAYWRIGHT

This play was written by me! I imagined all the characters and their story lines.

I am a
STAGEHAND

In the dark between scenes, I move the set around the stage.

I am an
USHER

The theater can be dark, so I show people to their seats with my little flashlight.

Welcome to the action!

Some jobs are full of adventure and can be dangerous, too. Often, the people who do them bravely put their own safety on the line to help others. They must stay fit and train for a long time to have the skills they need to stay safe. Many of these jobs used to be done by men only, but now lots of women do them, too, and they are just as good at them!

Who has an action-packed job?

I am in the
ARMY

I am in the army. I travel around the world in service of my country, to keep the peace.

I am in the
NAVY

I am in the navy. Instead of being on land, I defend my country by traveling the seas.

I am a
HELICOPTER
PILOT

I am the pilot of this helicopter. Helicopters don't need a runway like planes do—they can take off straight from the ground.

I am a
SECRET
AGENT

I have a secret mission, which I can't tell you about! I keep an eye on things and investigate to discover information.

I travel into space in my rocket! My mission is to explore our solar system to understand it better.

I investigate crimes and arrest criminals if they break the law.

When I hear there is a fire, I jump in my fire engine and race to the scene to put the fire out with my water hose.

I am a bit of a daredevil! I stand in for an actor and perform dangerous stunts in a film, like crashes, jumps, or fights.

Welcome to the hotel

If you are traveling to a new part of the world, you might stay in a hotel while you are there. Hotels can be huge—with rooms for hundreds of people—or just have a few rooms, but either way, everyone there will be working hard to make sure you eat well and have a good night's sleep before you go out to explore the next day. Bon voyage!

What do grown-ups do in a hotel?

I am the
HOTEL
MANAGER

I am the
RECEPTIONIST

I am in charge of the hotel, and I oversee all the people that work here.

I greet guests when they arrive at our hotel and help with their questions.

I am the
BELLHOP

I am the
CONCIERGE

Some people call me the porter. I am here to help you with your bags!

If you want to book tickets for a trip, ask me to make a reservation for you.

I am the
HOUSE-
KEEPER

I am the
CHEF

While you are out for the day, I make sure your room is clean and tidy.

Breakfast, lunch, and dinner—I cook them all for hundreds of guests every day!

I am the
WAITER

I am the
GUEST

I take your order and serve you your food at the restaurant. Bon appétit!

I am staying at the hotel on my trip away from home.

Welcome to the great outdoors!

You have to work indoors for lots of jobs...but not for all of them! Whether you prefer spending time at the beach, at the park, in the mountains, or even underwater, there's a job for you!

What do grown-ups do outdoors?

I am a
FISHERMAN

I am in the
COAST GUARD

I look out to sea to check that everyone's safe, and if someone is in trouble, I rescue them!

I sit on the waterfront with my rod to catch fish and sell them to be eaten.

I am a
WATER SPORTS
INSTRUCTOR

I am a
MARINE
BIOLOGIST

I teach people how to have fun in the water, surfing or windsurfing.

I study the wildlife in the sea, from the tiniest plankton to the biggest whale!

I am a
PARK
RANGER

I am a
TREE
SURGEON

I look after the park and the wildlife here, and I also give guided tours!

I make sure the trees are safe, and saw off any dangerous branches.

I am a
CONSERVATIONIST

I am an
OUTDOOR
ADVENTURE
INSTRUCTOR

I work to protect animals and the environment, and teach people about them.

I help people have fun outdoors—safely!—climbing and mountaineering.

Welcome to the concert hall

Some people are amazing singers, while others can play a musical instrument—if you want to see them perform, you can head to the lavish surroundings of the concert hall.

What do grown-ups do in the concert hall?

I am a
MUSICIAN

I am the
CONDUCTOR

I show the orchestra how slow (or fast!) and how quiet (or loud!) they should play.

I play a musical instrument and perform with the rest of the orchestra.

I am the
COMPOSER

I am an
OPERA
SINGER

My work is to sing with my beautiful voice. Sometimes a choir joins in, too.

I have written the music being played at this concert house!

I am the
BOX OFFICE
ASSISTANT

I am the
PHOTOGRAPHER

I am the photographer, here to take pictures of the musicians playing.

If you want to watch a performance, you can buy a ticket from me!

I am the
LIGHTING
TECHNICIAN

I am a MEMBER
OF THE
AUDIENCE

I control the lights in the concert hall, which can make the performance more dramatic.

I am here to enjoy the show and listen to the wonderful music!

Welcome to the newsroom

Every day, the news is broadcast on televisions to tell us about the important events happening around the world. On-screen, you might only see one or two presenters, but it takes a big team of people to investigate the facts and film the show. Take a look and see for yourself.

TV NEWS

What do grown-ups do in the newsroom?

I am the
NEWS
ANCHOR

I report the news—and I often help to research the facts and write the stories beforehand, too.

I am the
REPORTER

I am a journalist. I investigate stories and interview people.

I am the
POLITICIAN

I work for the government, and I'm here to talk about what I have been doing.

I am the
METEOROLOGIST

I gather scientific information to predict the weather for the week ahead.

I am the
CAMERA
OPERATOR

I am the
EDITOR

When we broadcast the news, I am behind the scenes, filming.

I gather the research together and decide what should be on the news that day.

I am the
PRODUCER

I am the
DIGITAL
EDITOR

I lead the film crew and am in control of everything as the program broadcasts.

I update the website and put news stories online.

Welcome to the gym

You might have noticed that a lot of jobs involve sitting down for long parts of the day...and that isn't good for staying fit and healthy! Because of this, lots of grown-ups head to the gym, to do classes and get active to make sure they stay in good shape.

What do grown-ups do in the gym?

I am the
GYM
INSTRUCTOR

I work out in the gym and help people improve their fitness.

I am the
DANCE
TEACHER

I give energetic dance classes – dancing is a fun way to keep active!

I am the
YOGA
INSTRUCTOR

I am the
PERSONAL
TRAINER

I show people the right way to stretch and move into different yoga positions.

I work one-to-one with people, encouraging them as they exercise.

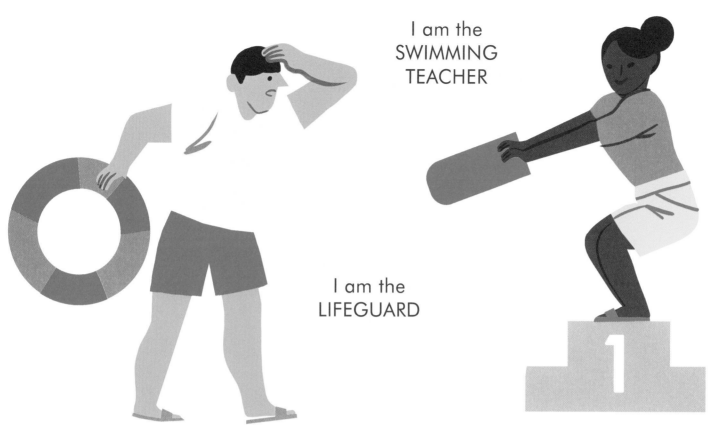

I am the
SWIMMING
TEACHER

I am the
LIFEGUARD

I keep watch by the pool and check that everyone in the water stays safe.

I teach people how to stay afloat in the water and become good swimmers.

I am the
MASSEUSE

I am the
MEMBER

People with sore muscles come to me and I soothe their pain with massage.

I come here to work out and keep my body fit. Exercising makes me feel good!

Welcome to the university

Many of the jobs in this book need the person doing it to understand and use difficult information, which goes beyond what they might have learned at school.

Universities are a place where grown-ups go to get this extra education from professors, who have studied their specific subject for years and years. You can study all kinds of things—take a look!

What do grown-ups do at the university?

I am the
PROVOST

I am the
OFFICE
ADMINISTRATOR

I make sure all the different departments are running smoothly.

I keep everyone who works here organized and in touch with each other.

I am the
CHEMISTRY
PROFESSOR

I am the
DOCTOR OF
ZOOLOGY

I research chemicals and materials, and help my students to study them, too.

I study animals and wildlife and give lectures to my students about them.

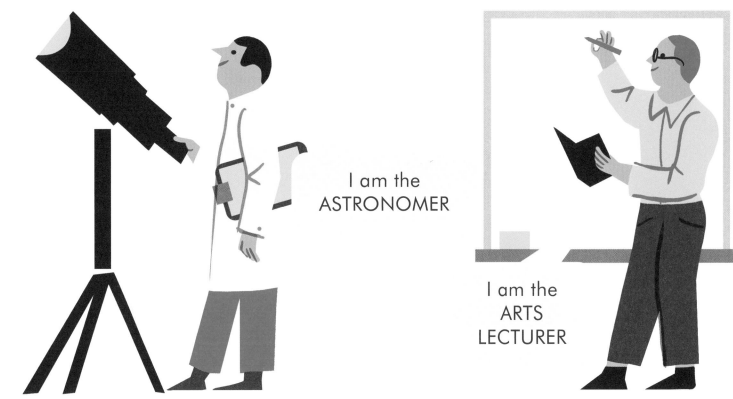

I am the
ASTRONOMER

I am the
ARTS
LECTURER

I think space is fascinating and use my research to explore new theories about it.

I am interested literature, art, and music, and teach my students about them.

I am the
ARTIST IN
RESIDENCE

I am the
STUDENT

I have been invited here to make art and inspire the students with my creativity.

I come to the university to learn, and will leave when I have completed my degree.

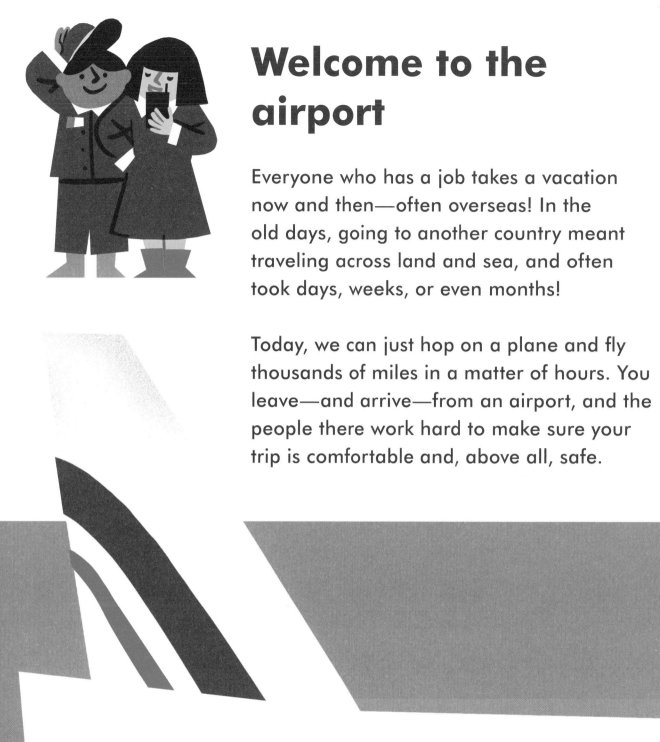

Welcome to the airport

Everyone who has a job takes a vacation now and then—often overseas! In the old days, going to another country meant traveling across land and sea, and often took days, weeks, or even months!

Today, we can just hop on a plane and fly thousands of miles in a matter of hours. You leave—and arrive—from an airport, and the people there work hard to make sure your trip is comfortable and, above all, safe.

What do grown-ups do at the airport?

I am the CAPTAIN

I am the COPILOT

I am in charge of everyone on the plane, and will safely fly you to your destination.

I am here to support the captain and help to fly the plane when he or she takes a break.

I am the FLIGHT ATTENDANT

I am the BAGGAGE HANDLER

Passenger safety is my number one priority as I look after you on board this plane.

I enjoy physical work! My job is to load and unload the passengers' luggage from the planes between flights.

I am a member of the CHECK-IN STAFF

I work in PASSPORT CONTROL

I book customers onto their flights and send their luggage to be loaded onto the right plane.

I check everyone's passport so that we know who is leaving and who is arriving in the country.

I am an AIR TRAFFIC CONTROLLER

I am a DOG HANDLER

I keep track of all the planes, making sure each one has enough space in the sky. The captain asks permission to land his or her plane from me.

My dog is specially trained to sniff out things that people aren't supposed to bring into the country.

61

Index

Actor	28	Decorator	21
Air traffic controller	61	Dentist	13
Ambulance driver	13	Director	28
Architect	20	Doctor	10–12
Army (see "Soldier")		Dog handler	61
Artist in residence	57	Drama teacher	9
Astronaut	33	Editor, digital (of news)	49
Astronomer	57	Editor (of news)	49
Audience member	45	Electrician	20
Baggage handler	60	Engineer	20
Baker	24	Farmer	14–16
Bellhop	36	Farmhand	17
Bookshop assistant	25	Firefighter	33
Box office assistant	45	Fisherman	40
Bricklayer	21	Flight attendant	60
Butcher	24	Florist	24
Camera operator	49	Gardener	17
Captain (pilot)	60	Guest (of a hotel)	37
Carpenter	21	Gym instructor	52
Check-in staff	62	Gym member	53
Chef	37	Gym teacher	8
Copilot	60	Hairdresser	25
Coast guard	40	Helicopter pilot	32
Composer	44	Hotel manager	36
Concierge	36	Housekeeper	37
Conductor	44	Laborer	21
Conservationist	41	Lecturer of arts	57
Costume designer	29	Librarian	8
Custodian	9	Lifeguard	53

Lighting technician	45		Politician	48
Makeup artist	28		Presenter, television	46–48
Marine biologist	40		Principal	8
Masseuse	53		Producer (news)	49
Mechanic	16		Professor of chemistry	56
Member, gym	53		Provost (university)	56
Meteorologist	48		Receptionist (hotel)	36
Milker	17		Reporter	48
Midwife	13		Sailor (see "Navy")	
Musician	44		Secret agent	32
Music teacher	9		Set designer	28
Navy	32		Shepherd	16
News anchor	48		Shop assistant	25
Nurse	10–12		Shopper	25
Office administrator	56		Soldier	32
Opera singer	44		Student (school)	9
Outdoor adventure instructor	41		Student (university)	57
Painter	21		Stuntman	33
Paramedic	13		Stagehand	29
Park ranger	41		Swimming teacher	53
Passport control	61		Teacher (school)	6-9
Personal trainer	52		Tractor driver	16
Pharmacist	12		Tree surgeon	41
Photographer	45		Usher	29
Physical therapist	12		Waiter	37
Pilot (see "Captain")			Water sports instructor	40
Playwright	29		Yoga instructor	52
Plumber	20		Zoology, doctor of	56
Police officer	33			

First published in the U.S. in 2016
by Wide Eyed Editions, an imprint of Quarto Inc.,
276 Fifth Avenue, Suite 206, New York, NY 10001
QuartoKnows.com
Visit our blogs at QuartoKnows.com

ISBN 978-1-84780-844-8

The illustrations were created digitally
Set in Futura

Designed by Andrew Watson
Edited by Jenny Broom
Published by Rachel Williams

Printed in China

3 5 7 9 8 6 4 2

FSC
www.fsc.org
MIX
Paper from
responsible sources
FSC® C104723